# FIVE MINUTES TO MIDNIGHT

## STORIES OF
## GOD'S FAITHFULNESS
## IN CENTRAL ASIA

### ANDREW SIEBERHAGEN

Five Minutes To Midnight
Stories of God's Faithfulness in Central Asia
Copyright © 2012 by Andrew Sieberhagen

Koozzz Publishing
Mount Vernon, Ohio 43050
www.koozzzpublishing.com

All rights reserved. No portion of this book may be reproduced in any form, stored, or transmitted in any form or by any means – electronic, mechanical, photocopy, recording, scanning, or other – except for the inclusion of brief quotations in a review or articles, without permission in writing from the author or publisher.

Cover Photo and Design by Koozzz Photographic
The Prodigal painting by an early believer in Central Asia.

Scripture taken from the Holy Bible, NEW INTERNATIONAL VERSION®. Copyright © 1973, 1978, 1984 by Biblica, Inc. All rights reserved worldwide. Used by permission.

NEW INTERNATIONAL VERSION® and NIV® are registered trademarks of Biblica, Inc. Use of either trademark for the offering of goods or services requires the prior written consent of Biblica US, Inc.

Italics and bold formatting added by the author for emphasis.

---

ISBN-13: 978-0-9830760-4-9
ISBN-10: 0983076049
Library of Congress Control Number: 2012931827

As you read these insightful sketches of two people willing to pay the price and trust God through the difficulties of cross cultural mission, your heart will be stirred and your faith challenged. Through Andrew's vulnerable honesty, you will be inspired to trust God for more and moved to do more for God.

Peter Nicoll, CEO<br>OM Ships International

---

The old adage "smooth seas never made a good sailor" is what this book is very much about; how to "sail" God's boat in the world's stormy waters. The world we live in, with its many distractions and vain pursuits, can so easily 'choke us out'. This book is a usable manual in learning to be good sailors!

Abd-ul-Haqq

---

Fasten your seat belt and get ready for the ride of your life as you follow Andy and Lynn on their Central Asian adventures. This book will inspire and motivate you to go and get your own stories.

Julyan Lidstone, OM

I'm sure the idea of going to a distant land to share Christ with those who have never heard can sound like a real adventure. It would be easy to envision all kinds of exciting experiences and challenging opportunities that would thrill any heart as well as stretch your faith. But for these newlyweds it wasn't the adventure or even the opportunity that compelled them to step, it was something much more.

*Five Minutes to Midnight* reveals the real motivation and drive behind Andy and Lynn's call to the mission field. It's the same thing that continues to press them forward even now, while serving in the local church. It's the possibility of a fresh encounter with the living God. *"If your Presence does not go with us, do not send us up from here."* (Exodus 33:15) Their stories not only confirm God's faithfulness to them but will also ignite your own soul to step out for God so that you might encounter His glory.

Jim Zippay, Lead Pastor
Heritage Christian Church, Westerville, Ohio

# DEDICATION

To my beautiful wife
who dared to trust God
as we lived among
the unreached.

# Acknowledgements

Lynn, the love of my life,
for your edits and contributions
to the early drafts.

Mom & Dad, for your wisdom
and manuscript edits... and for
being simply amazing to me.

Jeff, for your direction and encouragement;
this would not have happened without you.

My fellow workers throughout the years.

One of the first Central Asian believers, for your
painting of the prodigal son used on the cover; it's a
reflection of my journey as I often collapsed into the
arms of my Heavenly Father... who never let go!

Jesus, because apart from you I can't do anything.

# Table of Contents

Foreword: Abd-ul-Haqq: .................................. 11
Introduction: Andrew Sieberhagen: ................... 13
1. Am I Not Sending You?: ............................. 15
2. In The Deep: ............................................. 19
3. The Wolf Will Live With The Lamb: ........... 23
4. Prepare The Bride: .................................... 27
5. Porcupines On Sunday: ............................. 33
6. The Bread Of Heaven: ............................... 37
7. Midnight Injections: .................................. 41
8. Expect The Unexpected: ............................ 45
9. Treasure In A Field: .................................. 49
10. Love Your Enemy: .................................... 53
11. The Angel From South Africa: ................... 57
12. Some Fish And A Few Loaves: .................. 61
13. Just As You Are: ...................................... 67
14. The Weekend That Changed Everything: ... 73

15. Grace Awakening: ............................................. 77
16. Seventy Times Seven: ..................................... 81
17. They Walk With God: ..................................... 85
18. A Refugee In Turkey: ..................................... 89
19. The Novice Smuggler: ................................... 95
20. Waiting Is The Hardest Part: ...................... 101
21. Getting To The Other Side: ........................ 107
22. Our Central Asian Child: ............................ 111
23. Up In Smoke: ............................................... 117
24. A Healing Planned 100 Years Ago: ........... 123
25. A Dream Come True: ................................. 129
26. Love Is A Verb: ............................................ 133
27. Who Are You?: ............................................ 137
28. The Macedonian Call: ................................. 143
29. Waiting All This Time: ................................ 147
30. Angels Unaware: .......................................... 151

# Foreword

If you ever have the chance to sit with Andy & Lynn Sieberhagen, it will strike you immediately that they understand what is important; see things others do not see; and are willing to be change agents, taking initiative to do what needs to be done.

Thus this book. It is real! It is them! Central Asia may not be your setting, but the lessons they had to learn are relevant for all of us, whatever context.

The Sieberhagens are not interested in any way to make names for themselves. They simply have a heart for people, to bring them truth that they might be set free, to empower them to move forward, whatever their nation, situation or struggle.

The old adage "smooth seas never made a good sailor" is what this book is very much about; how to "sail" God's boat in the world's stormy waters…

The world we live in, with its many distractions and vain pursuits, can so easily 'choke us out'. This book is a usable manual in learning to be good sailors!

Abd-ul-Haqq

# Introduction

Throughout biblical history the Jewish nation had a tradition of putting memorial stones in places where God had clearly met with them or come to their rescue. These stones served as reminders to them and to the generations that followed that God is faithful.

As I reflect on the ten years spent in Central Asia with my family, I am overwhelmed by the memories of how faithful God was to us so many times. He often showed up at five minutes to midnight but... He showed up! Had He not, we would never have made it out there.

I felt a need to document some of these events so that we, as a family, would not forget them. I also thought it would be an encouragement to those who stood with us in support all those years and prayed for us through the tough times.

My hope is that anyone reading these stories will have a renewed trust in the God who is faithful, and learn to wait on Him even if it is five minutes to midnight.

When we take time to remember the past we have greater faith to trust Him for the future, and in so doing, attempt even greater things for Him

# CHAPTER 1

# AM I NOT SENDING YOU?

*The LORD turned to him and said, "Go in the strength you have and save Israel out of Midian's hand. Am I not sending you?"*

*Judges 6:14*

## March 1999

Following our wedding we were advised to spend a year at home together before going to the mission field. That wise counsel proved very valuable as we entered into what we were sure was to be marital bliss.

Marriage is a wonderful place. It reveals the true self of a person—the self that needs to be at the altar every day. During our first year of marriage I learned much about myself and how selfish I really was. I was very grateful for the time God spent working on that part of me along with all the other areas that I wasn't even aware of.

This was to be quite a year for us in many ways as we began making preparations to leave. My appendix had burst which I have since realized would have been my death had I already been in Central Asia… getting married literally saved my life! More concerning was the discovery that my wife was prone to kidney infections and that over the years there had already been some damage to them. Following a hospital procedure we were confident that the problem was corrected and continued making plans to leave. Bladder infections were more frequent than we had anticipated but we remained hopeful.

Our sending agency required us to attend training prior to leaving and it was during the final week of training that we encountered another setback, a major kidney infection.

## Chapter 1: Am I Not Sending You?

With our tickets purchased and in the final stages of planning I remember feeling hopeless, frustrated and angry all at the same time. I took a long walk into the field and had it out with God. "Surely not now! We have come so far! What must we do? Can we go?" I had my Bible and randomly opened it to chapter six of the book of Judges, not something I often do or recommend. What could Judges possibly have for me? Reluctantly I read the chapter and discovered HIS WORD for us in verse 14. *"...Go in the strength you have... Am I not sending you?"* Wow! That sealed the deal right then and there. I returned and told my wife that we had the green light and that we were going. Little did we know how critical that WORD would be for the adventures and challenges that awaited us.

As for the kidney infection, a visit to the doctor and a prescription for antibiotics took care of it before we left.

I am thankful we do not know what tomorrow holds. If we did I'm not sure we would ever take a risk for God, forever questioning whether we had what it takes to make it through anything and everything that He puts before us.

I have heard it said that "we should never waste today's grace on imaginations that do not exist. God promises us enough grace for today!" Now many years later as I write this I can say that there will be times you may have to hold on with all that you have, BUT... God does enable and provide for everything we will need in order for us to thrive in what He has called us to do.

## POINTS TO PONDER:
- Just because I'm *called* doesn't mean everything will go smoothly.
- His Word is true no matter what the circumstances are or what others tell you. Choose to believe and then take the RISKS.
- Faith is spelled R-I-S-K!

# Chapter 2

# In The Deep

*The LORD had said to Abram, "Leave your country, your people and your father's household and go to the land I will show you. I will make you into a great nation and I will bless you; I will make your name great, and you will be a blessing. I will bless those who bless you, and whoever curses you I will curse; and all peoples on earth will be blessed through you."*

*Genesis 12:1-3*

## April 1999

We boarded the plane with some tears, having said goodbye to family and friends, and yet we were excited. We were heading to a land that we had never been to before so we could live among a people we had only read about. A hidden Muslim people group discovered after the fall of Communism. Why there? Very simply, Jesus commands us to GO to all nations, and this was a nation of unreached people. Central Asia had opened up to the world and there was an opportunity to get in. People have complicated the term *calling* and have neglected to go where the needs are so great.

On a stopover in Turkey we discovered that the hotel we were staying at was filled with pilgrims returning from Mecca. Needless to say we stood out from the crowd. We discovered some were from South Africa and friendly conversation followed. When they asked where we were going we told them we were going to do humanitarian work among the Central Asian people. After making sure we understood that the people we were going to help were Muslim they wished us success there! We gladly accepted their wishes.

We landed in the capital city—innocent, wide-eyed and clueless—at 5:00 a.m. We were launched into the "expect the worst and you can only be surprised" world of pioneer missions. We made our way through customs with all our baggage only to discover that there was no one to pick us up. There were about 200 taxi drivers fighting for our business so we stayed inside. I had a telephone number but

CHAPTER 2: IN THE DEEP

there were no public phones at the airport. Finally, a **security guard** took pity on us and escorted us to the only phone around; it was a wind-up model located in the car parking lot. Thankfully our driver on the other end answered and came to pick us up; he had mistaken our arrival date.

*Ready to Go!*

Our original plans were to spend a year learning the ropes with my brother before heading to another city to begin a new work. However, God's ways are not our ways! Due to medical issues he and his family were getting ready to leave the country, so following our arrival we said goodbye to them. Though we were suddenly placed into the hands of people we had never met, we now realize that we were always safely in the hands of the One who never lets us go, and it has all worked out.

## Points To Ponder:

- The mandate Jesus gave was for us to GO and make disciples of all nations! This means that there is no "calling" needed to go, if anything, the "calling" is required to stay.
- In the world of missions, expect the unexpected.
- We can plan all we want but He wants us to be in the palm of His hands. Sometimes that means He takes away the safety nets we put up before we jump.

# CHAPTER 3

# THE WOLF WILL LIVE WITH THE LAMB

*The wolf will live with the lamb, the leopard will lie down with the goat, the calf and the lion and the yearling together; and a little child will lead them.*

*Isaiah 11:6*

## June 1999

The moment we had been dreading had arrived. There is no better way to effectively learn a new language and adapt to a new culture than to move in with a local family—at least that's what they told us. We had been in country for about one week, and it was time to make that move.

Our teammate led us into a valley where we entered the heart of the old city. It was a maze of houses leading into each other with little roads for getting in and out. We were welcomed into the home of a local owner whom we had never met. His name was Faruq, and he spoke no English. Our teammate helped negotiate the rent, wished us well, and left.

Our field preparation did not include any form of sign language training, yet that was the only form of communication we had in those early days.

We were shown to a little whitewashed room in the corner of the courtyard which was to become our home for the next four months. There were some floor mattresses and some privacy—what more does one need? The washroom consisted of a bucket located in a steam room at the bottom of the house, and the toilet was a hole in the ground across from us. It didn't take long to discover that coughing was the signal to make sure you didn't walk in on anyone. Living with scorpions was never mentioned when we signed up either; in fact, there were many things that were not mentioned.

## Chapter 3: The Wolf Will Live With The Lamb

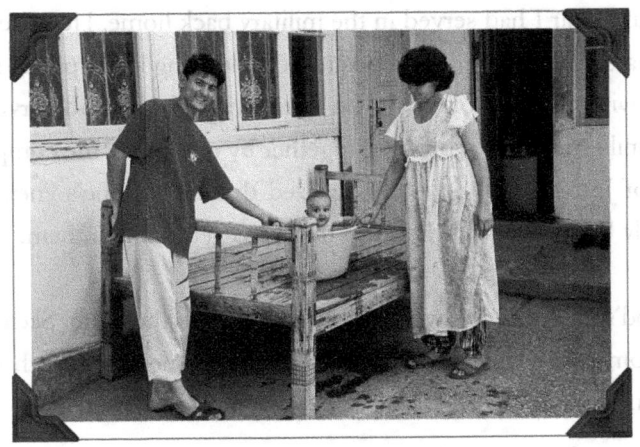

*Our Host Family*

We started to connect with the family by using cards, music and photos to get through those first evenings. When I asked our host what kind of music he liked, he pulled out a Boney M record and put it on the turntable. Here was Boney M singing "Mary's Boy Child Jesus Christ was born on Christmas Day..." loud enough for the entire neighborhood to hear. My wife and I looked at each other wondering what to make of it. They had no clue what was being sung, but that night, the name of Jesus was spoken over an entire neighborhood of Muslims who had never heard the gospel. It seemed like Faruq was to be God's messenger until we, the church, would bring the gospel!

I soon discovered that Faruq had served in the Communist Navy the same year I had served in the military back home. Here we were, ten years after serving on opposite sides, looking at his photo album filled with pictures of Lenin on the naval ship he had served on. Two military enemies brought together by one thing, the compelling love of Jesus for all people. I realized that loving one's enemy can actually be pretty easy when you decide to get to know them.

In God's kingdom the wolf is able to live with the lamb. Seeing His kingdom come to all parts of the earth is something worth giving your life for.

## POINTS TO PONDER:
- Jesus is the bridge between love and hate.
- His love makes the impossible possible.
- Your enemy may not be as bad as you think.
- If it has flesh and blood it's not your enemy anyway.

# Chapter 4

# Prepare The Bride

*Let us rejoice and be glad and give him glory! For the wedding of the Lamb has come, and his bride has made herself ready.*

*Revelation 19:7*

## July 1999

Summer is traditionally wedding season and a huge highlight in the community. We were quite excited when our host family invited us to attend a family wedding with them. It would be a good way to learn more of the culture and strengthen our relationship with them.

We left for the village at about 10:00 a.m. on a Friday morning thinking it would probably be a long day before we returned home. We had no clue what we were in for.

We had only been in the country for about a month and were not yet fluent in the language. We arrived with wedding preparations in full swing and other guests were also arriving. My wife and I were shown to separate seats as is the common practice there. There had probably never been foreigners from Africa in the village before and we were treated like celebrities; everyone wanted to talk with us.

It was great to talk with the other guests, at least for the first few minutes, after that they would carry on even though we told them we didn't understand. Eventually we just began saying yes to everything; which we would later learn can get you into trouble.
Because the bride was from our side of the family we were to host the wedding on this particular day and await the coming of the groom. We were learning much about the wedding culture there.

CHAPTER 4: PREPARE THE BRIDE

The groom would arrive sometime in the evening. He would be preceded by trumpeters heralding his arrival and making sure that the bride was ready. A busload of guests would accompany the groom and then a celebration with the bride's family would take place before he departed for the night.

*Announcing the Arrival of the Groom*

My wife and I spent the entire day sitting and waiting. Our hosts kept asking whether we were bored. (Of course, even if we were, you could never say that to the host). Finally the trumpets sounded and things started to get exciting.

One tradition is for guests to offer messages to the bride and groom wishing them well... and then to dance for them. It seemed like a wonderful idea—until we were the ones asked to give the message and dance, local style, in front of 200 other guests. I struggle to dance in front of my wife! Thankfully we had the opportunity to watch others first.

*Our First Wedding Dance*

I imagined that I was an airplane, with my arms stretched out wide and flying with rhythm! It seemed to be acceptable because people came and put money in our pockets and under our hats; they even wrapped scarves around us. When the song was over I walked off thinking how generous these people were. Soon, someone tapped my shoulder and said that the money was for the musicians. The entire evening was a fun experience.

## Chapter 4: Prepare The Bride

The groom finally left late into the night and we began preparing to go home. It was then that we were told we would be staying the night. I slept in a room with ten male guests, while my wife stayed in another room with some women. We survived the night thinking that we would return home the next morning... not so!

We were then invited to the house of the groom later in the day to celebrate with his side of the family! It was a long day of waiting, made more difficult because we were unable to communicate with anyone.

We finally boarded a crowded bus and headed to the groom's home along with the bride and her guests. Upon arriving, the groom approached the bus, picked up the bride and carried her over his shoulder into the house. So began another huge celebration.

We spoke, stood, sat, danced, received money, gave money, and then went home, but not *our* home—but back to the home of the bride for another night.

It was now Sunday and we were cross-eyed with culture shock. Desperate, I approached our host and asked whether he could take us home. Six hours later we arrived back at our little whitewashed room. For a few brief hours it felt like our own five-star room on Paradise Island!

It was an unforgettable experience that taught us so much about the people we had come to love and serve, but it also provided great lessons on what we would and would not do at future weddings. As I reflected on the wedding traditions I had just experienced, I realized how rich they were with biblical images. For the first time I got a sense of what it means to *prepare* for Jesus' coming, to *celebrate* His coming, and then to see Him *come* for His bride with all the excitement and expectation of the occasion. I can't wait for that day.

## Points To Ponder:

- God places redemptive keys or symbols into all cultures that can be used by workers to point people toward Him.
- There is a wedding being prepared that is worth getting excited about.
- *"And this gospel of the kingdom will be preached in the whole world as a testimony to all nations, and then the end will come"* ~ Matthew 24:14
- The Groom is preparing to return.

# CHAPTER 5

# PORCUPINES ON SUNDAY

*...And I pray that you, being rooted and established in love, may have power, together with all the saints, to grasp how wide and long and high and deep is the love of Christ, and to know this love that surpasses knowledge—that you may be filled to the measure of all the fullness of God.*

*Ephesians 3:17-19*

## AUGUST 1999

It was 45 degrees Celsius in the shade on a Sunday afternoon. We had been in the country for three months living with a local family, wondering when we would ever begin to grasp the language.

There was not much going on that day; in fact the highlight was the arrival of Jalaramis. That was the name we gave to a chicken from the community who had flown into the courtyard. She had decided to use the clay oven outside our room to lay her eggs.

I was bored out of my mind... language learning! Five new words that day, and I had to get them to stick in my brain. What bothered me most was that it was easy to remember words that were not important, while the words I really needed to know would take forever to learn.

Our language teacher told us a story about a porcupine, which is a complicated ten letter word in the local language. By the end of the story there was only one word that stuck with me... ***porcupine***! The funny thing is that they don't even have porcupines there.

I found myself in a real negative place, feeling like I would never learn the language, second-guessing myself, wondering why I ever decided to come to this place; it was almost like a completely different planet. To top it off our return airline tickets to our home country had expired!

CHAPTER 5: PORCUPINES ON SUNDAY

When I was involved in ministry back home it felt like I was really making a difference; here, I felt like a burden to everyone.

There I was, like Jonah, sitting in the shade of a tree having my pity party with God. I was desperate to hear from Him and called out … and He answered!

I heard him ask questions like "Where am I right now?" and "Who is the source of your fullness and contentment?" I was humbled. I hadn't realized how spiritually bankrupt I was. There I was, a *noble* young man who had left everything to come and live among these people, and yet the very foundation of my faith was misplaced. My relationship with God was wonderful when ministry and circumstances were going well, but when things were not going well my relationship suffered. I realized that Jesus was not the source of my fulfillment, the work I was doing for Him was. That day was a game changer for me!

The King of Kings and Creator of the universe was in the middle of my life, He had never left. He was my source of life and needed to be my fulfillment regardless of my situation.

I resolved to move the foundation of my life that day from the sand to the ROCK! Even if I spent the rest of my life in this place without seeing fruit it would not affect the fullness and fulfillment that I have in Christ. He was to be my source… and He never changes!

I was on a new journey that liberated me from the need to perform for His favor and acceptance—a journey I am still on today.

## POINTS TO PONDER:

- Understanding and believing the extent of His love for me is the key to fullness.
- Nothing I do or don't do will make Him love me any more or less.
- Jesus, not what I do for Him, is the Source of fullness of life.
- Freedom from the need to perform in order to be accepted is a wonderful thing.

# CHAPTER 6

# THE BREAD OF HEAVEN

*Jesus answered, "It is written: 'Man does not live on bread alone, but on every word that comes from the mouth of God.'"*

*Matthew 4:4*

## September 1999

Dilbahar was an amazingly committed language teacher and a strong Muslim. Learning the language is vital in the early stage of adapting to a new culture, and the goal is to try to get 40 hours of practical study in each week for as long as possible. I set aside Fridays to learn religious terms and phrases. This soon became the place where faith issues were hotly debated. As a Muslim, she believes that both the Bible and the Koran are holy books from God. Where there are any contradictions, the Koran overrules because she believes the Bible has been changed.

Following several debates, I challenged her by saying that there was no way for both books to be from God because there are simply too many fundamental differences. I told her that one of them must be false! Dilbahar did not appreciate that comment, and with the New Testament in her hand she reached out her arm and asked me a rather devastating question. She said, "Okay, let's say that the Bible is the true book from God. How was my grandfather ever meant to find the truth? He lived and died having never seen a word of the Bible in his language. We have had the Koran for all these years. So... if the Bible is the Word of God, why is it still not in our language?" What would you say in a moment like that? "Dilbahar," I answered, "please forgive us, who have had this for so long in our language, for not bringing it to you sooner."

I left feeling rather ashamed. I couldn't help thinking of how many Bible translations we have in English. How do we justify so many

## Chapter 6: The Bread Of Heaven

when there are still thousands of languages in the world without the scriptures? Daniel Webster said, "If we abide by the principles taught in the Bible, our country will go on prospering...." So what does a nation do that does not have the Bible in its language?

This experience impacted me deeply. In one sense, I was grateful to have been born and raised with the scriptures; they have been a compass providing true direction for my life. But I was also burdened by how many resources the western church spends on itself when the mandate to go and make disciples of all nations is so clear.

Things have since begun to change. Nonwestern nations are beginning to experience God in unprecedented ways and becoming more mission-minded themselves. The face of today's missionary is also changing. Bible translators have been able to identify the tasks that remain and are setting goals to begin translation work for every language by 2030. May we, the Church, rise up to this glorious challenge. *"Man does not live on bread alone but on every word that comes from the mouth of God"* (Matthew 4:4).

## POINTS TO PONDER:

- There are approximately 2,000 languages today without the scriptures.
- How many Bibles and versions do you have in your language?
- Do you cherish the scriptures?
- Is there anything you can do to help get the scriptures into every language on earth?

# CHAPTER 7

# MIDNIGHT INJECTIONS

*He who dwells in the shelter of the Most High will rest in the shadow of the Almighty. I will say of the LORD, "He is my refuge and my fortress, my God, in whom I trust."*

*If you make the Most High your dwelling— even the LORD, who is my refuge— then no harm will befall you, no disaster will come near your tent.*

*Psalm 91:1-2; 9-10*

## April 2000

Following the completion of our apprenticeship training in leadership and church planting, we packed up our little car with all that we owned and headed to the city God was calling us to. We were joining a brand-new team, and it felt good to finally be settling into a place and context we could call and make our own. After being there for just two weeks, my wife woke me around midnight and said she had a kidney infection, and that it was getting worse.

It was the middle of the night in a city where we knew no doctors. Now what were we to do? I grabbed my Bible and opened it up to the reading for that day and just began to read it out loud. It was Psalm 91. As I read it, each verse seemed to describe our situation; *"He is my refuge and my fortress, my God in whom I trust." Surely he will save you from the fowler's snare and from the deadly pestilence... You will not fear the terror of night... nor the pestilence that stalks in the darkness... no harm will befall you... he will command his angels... to guard you in all your ways"* It was as though God was in the room speaking directly to us. I closed the Bible and told my wife that no matter what happens, God is here and knows about this. I picked up the phone and called the only doctor we knew in another city. Miraculously, he answered the phone, gave us the name of the medication to get and told us to locate a pharmacy.

## Chapter 7: Midnight Injections

I remembered seeing a pharmacy about one mile away and only hoped it would be open. By His grace it was, but now I faced a new challenge—how to communicate with the pharmacist, who didn't speak the same language that we had learned. I tried every version I knew in order to make him understand what medication we needed but with no success. I went home and returned with my wife to try and convince him of what we needed for her. When *she* pronounced the name of the medication, he recognized it (though I was certain I had pronounced it that way). He gave us five little bottles, along with five injection needles. For someone who doesn't like needles, I would now be injecting a significant amount of antibiotic into my wife at 2:00 in the morning. At this point, the thought of having me administer an injection was more frightening to her than the kidney infection. It was a good distraction.

We made it through the night and gave God the praise for providing the antibiotics that killed the infection. Once again God had brought us through what seemed like an impossible situation.

## Points To Ponder:

- Healing doesn't always come in the way we ask for.
- He is there with us in the darkest of places.
- Pray, believe in His presence, and do everything you can.
- The Word is alive, and Psalm 91 is true.

# CHAPTER 8

# EXPECT THE UNEXPECTED

*That is why, for Christ's sake, I delight in weaknesses, in insults, in hardships, in persecutions, in difficulties. For when I am weak, then I am strong.*

*2 Corinthians 12:10*

## April 2000

Our first church planting team was made up of a Korean, an American, a Chinese, an Afrikaner, a Brit, and two English-speaking South Africans. There was no doubt that when this team met boredom would not be an issue!

Before moving to the city the team went away for a strategy weekend to discuss what we believed God's will was for us there. We were excited and motivated as we left, feeling that God had put together a team with multiple gifts.

I would be leading the team and church planting efforts, while another would head up the development work. We were in the country on humanitarian aid visas that required 20 hours of work each week. One of the workers already had a commitment of $15,000 toward the development work. Things were in place for a great start to the work... or so I thought.

A faithful couple who had served in the city for some years gave me some wise counsel as they were leaving. They said there had been three teams that had tried to start a work there previously and that the enemy had successfully destroyed each of them. They stressed for us to be on our guard because we might be next!

It turned out that no team had lasted more than two years in this particular city. At our first meeting, we agreed to meet every day to pray during the first month.

## Chapter 8: Expect The Unexpected

We had been together for two weeks when I received a call around 11:00 p.m. from one of my team members, insisting that I come to his place right away. On my way there, I was nervous and braced myself for bad news. He was in the midst of a crisis and within two weeks returned to his home country permanently along with the $15,000 we had been counting on. Our first casualty!

As the team leader, I felt as though I was in way too deep, deeper than anything I had experienced before. But I was determined to see a beachhead established in this city for God's kingdom! I concluded that the only way for anything to be accomplished there was to be because of and by Jesus!

I certainly felt helpless, but God was faithful! He sent us a short-term worker from Zimbabwe who would turn out to be a full-time intercessor! God heard our prayers and saw the desperation in our hearts. So began a season of hard work, team perseverance, wrestling with the enemy, and the miracle work of a God who loves us and the people we had come to serve.

Our team was able to do a faithful work during the next eight years until all foreign workers were asked to leave. More accurately, until God decided that our part in building His kingdom in that city had come to a close.

## POINTS TO PONDER:
- Satan is out to steal and destroy God's people, and in this realm, ignorance is not bliss.
- The keys to effective kingdom building are brokenness and humility.
- When I am weak, He is strong.
- If you don't get out of the boat, you will never know what it is like to walk on water.

# Chapter 9

# Treasure In A Field

*"The kingdom of heaven is like treasure hidden in a field. When a man found it, he hid it again, and then in his joy went and sold all he had and bought that field."*

*Matthew 13:44*

## July 2000

Communicating is a crucial element to reaching people with the gospel, so learning their heart language is vital. Since resources for learning the language were not readily available we found ourselves dependent upon local language helpers.

Odil was a great teacher who made a huge difference in my language training. We met three times a week for two hours at a time. We were able to build a strong friendship, which provided the opportunity for us to talk about Jesus. Even though he was a Muslim, our friendship had grown to the point of praying for each other at the end of our lessons. He seemed to be open to the things of God, and I felt as though he was really beginning to understand the truths of the gospel.

One day I asked him whether he was ready to start following Jesus. He told me that he really needed to be sure before he could accept what I was telling him because it might cost him everything. Becoming a follower of Christ could cost him his friends and family, and he might not ever be able to get a job or get married.

I returned home and went through a personal faith crisis for several days. For the first time in my life I was faced with presenting the gospel to someone where it could actually cost him everything to follow Jesus, something I had never faced myself.

## Chapter 9: Treasure In A Field

Back home, following Jesus was not a difficult decision. The only possible cost might be to a person's pride. People at home were aware that I was prepared to leave everything to come and serve in this place, but the truth was that at any point I had the option to get on a plane and return home. For these people, however, once they chose to follow Jesus, that was it; there was no turning back.

I remember having a moment with God when I questioned Him, saying, "God, this message had better be true because if it isn't, then why on earth am I here and what am I asking these people to do?" I know it sounds crazy that a missionary would ask something like that; it's just that while I had always believed it, I had never faced this sort of reality. I had been in the country for two years and was only now starting to get a good perspective on how people lived.

When I compared the life I had been living with Christ to the life Odil was living without Christ, there was no comparison. He had been raised in a society without the gospel or a witness to the truths of God or to the moral and spiritual costs of living without Him.

It was then that I knew, without a doubt, that following Jesus was a price worth paying no matter the cost.

It was an important encounter for me because I had gained the confidence in my own spirit to tell Odil or anyone else the truth.

*"The kingdom of God is like a treasure in a field. When a man found it, he hid it again, and then in his joy went and sold all that he had and bought the field."* Now I get it.

## POINTS TO PONDER:
- There is a treasure to be found that no money can buy.
- Have you found the treasure? Have you sold the field?
- It cost Jesus everything.
- *"...any of you who does not give up everything he has cannot be my disciple."* ~ Luke 14:33

# CHAPTER 10

# LOVE YOUR ENEMY

> *"But I tell you: Love your enemies and pray for those who persecute you..."*
>
> Matthew 5:44

## AUGUST 2000

Our Central Asian country is a huge cotton-producing nation. Each year in August, the government closes all educational institutions and government offices to send everyone out to pick cotton. Every morning and evening there is a convoy of buses as far as the eye can see transporting pickers back and forth to the fields.

On one particular evening, I was returning home with a group of new field workers that had joined our team. We came to a stoplight, and when the light showed green, I turned. A policeman at the light signaled for me to stop. Note that in this part of the world, the police are not always friendly and will look for reasons to extort money from you. He checked my documents and then informed me that I had driven through a red light. Attempting to avoid an embarrassing situation with our new workers anxiously looking on, I insisted that I had not. While we were arguing, a convoy of buses began arriving at the intersection from picking cotton that day. The policeman was on duty at the stoplight and dropped my documents on the ground to run back to manage traffic. I figured this was the best time to make our getaway…. I mean since we would be waiting a long time for the convoy to drive through, I decided it would be in everyone's best interest that we leave rather than block traffic. So I got back in the car and drove off.

## Chapter 10: Love Your Enemy

A few minutes later I spotted a car speeding up from behind flashing for me to stop. It was him… Darth Vader! In this country, police carry red batons that look like light sabers to pull innocent people like me over! I realized that I had now created some very significant trouble for myself. I tried to explain to him that since he had dropped my documents I thought we were done, but that didn't work. He then asked the question the police seem to always ask, "What are we going to do about this?" In other words, how much are you going to pay me to get out of this? I took a chance and suggested that he stop by our home for a meal. I told him how good my wife had become in preparing some of the local dishes. I could tell he had never heard that one before, so I invited him again and to my surprise he asked when he should stop by.

The next night, he was sitting in our home enjoying a meal and singing local songs with us. As it turned out, he was a wedding singer when not on duty as a policeman. A few months later, he invited my wife and I to his wedding in the village. When we arrived we were given the place of honor next to him at the wedding table on the stage. Below us sat about 300 policemen dressed in uniform, a daunting sight to say the least. That night I made every effort to make sure that they remembered our faces and understood that we were friends with this officer. It was sure to save us a lot of stress in the days ahead.

## Points To Ponder:

- When we initiate an expression of God's love to someone we regard as our enemy it opens the way for a divine transformation to take place.
- Choosing to express love rather than hate has a way of disarming even the worst of enemies.
- There is one power greater than hate, and that is love.
- Love has a name… Jesus!

# CHAPTER 11

# THE ANGEL FROM SOUTH AFRICA

*My help comes from the Lord, the Maker of heaven and earth. He will not let your foot slip—he who watches over you will not slumber;*

*Psalm 121:2-3*

## October 2000

Once each quarter we would travel to the capital city for a short break. We had been in country for 18 months, and it was good to visit with some of the other workers, including my parents, who were serving in the same country.

On this visit my wife was struggling with an infection that had persisted for a number of weeks. Several antibiotics were administered but with no success. We were both very discouraged and I had reached the point of assuring her that if something didn't change by morning we would make arrangements to travel back home.

It was one of those moments where I gave up and surrendered it over to God, saying "We have done everything we can, God! Unless you do something in the next 12 hours, we will have to return home." Mentally I was already making travel plans and considering the implications of heading back home.

My mother returned home from an event she had attended with some other South African workers. She explained that she had been washing dishes with **a woman who had just arrived in the country**. When my mom shared our medical struggles with her, she turned and said, "You are describing the same type of symptoms my daughter has been experiencing." She went on to say that a new drug had been discovered that was working better than any they had

## Chapter 11: The Angel From South Africa

tried before. She handed some to my mom and told her to take them home to see whether they would help my wife.

That evening she took the medication. We prayed, and then went to sleep. When she awoke the next morning she was already feeling better than she had felt in weeks, and soon was infection free.

God sent an angel to us from South Africa at the exact time of our need. Once again I sat marveling at how our Father met our need as the clock was striking midnight. We went on to serve another eight years in Central Asia after that night.

## Points To Ponder:
- Sometimes we have to wait until the strike of midnight for Him to rescue us.
- God definitely uses medicine as an agent of healing.
- Only in heaven will we see the roles that angels played throughout our lives on earth.
- He is faithful to His promises even when it doesn't seem like it.

# FIVE MINUTES TO MIDNIGHT



60

# CHAPTER 12

# SOME FISH AND A FEW LOAVES

> *Taking the five loaves and the two fish and looking up to heaven, he gave thanks and broke the loaves. Then he gave them to his disciples to set before the people. He also divided the two fish among them all. They all ate and were satisfied...*
>
> *Mark 6:41-42*

## June 2001

During our first year of work in the city we taught English at the University and Technical Institute, as well as running an English library there. Since we were the only native English speakers, our library proved very popular.

One day the vice rector of the University came to us and said they had other plans for the space we were using and that we would have to move. I suggested to the team that the time had come for us to establish a place of our own from which we could do development work. So we began to pray.

The head of the University said that we would never be able to attract students to an off-campus site, but we pressed on. One day a local friend pointed out a rather large house for sale situated in a nearby neighborhood. When we went to look at the space, I immediately visualized how it would be setup; it was ideal for our needs. We agreed to buy it for $4,500 though we realized it would require an additional $15,000 to convert it into a development center.

Through prayer and communicating the need to our supporters, we were able to raise enough to purchase the property. Obtaining permission to work in the area and registering the center in the name of our NGO seemed highly unlikely, though. Considering that the local government in this country did not normally allow such things, the possibility of gaining approval seemed remote at best.

## CHAPTER 12: SOME FISH AND A FEW LOAVES

Amazingly we located an attorney willing to put the property in our name. To complete the registration process, a face-to-face meeting with the local mayor was required.

Odil, my local language helper, was critical in helping us get our development work off the ground. He and I had made good progress in talking about faith and would end our language sessions in prayer. He had grown in faith to where his prayers to God had become personal.

For weeks we had tried, unsuccessfully, to make an appointment with the mayor. One day as we were about to leave for the mayor's office, Odil said he knew why we weren't able to see the mayor; it was because we hadn't prayed before going!

You can imagine how humbled I was by that, so we bowed and prayed for God's favor. Fifteen minutes later we were sitting in the office of the most powerful man in the city. Thirty minutes later, we walked out with signed papers granting us permission to register the center and begin our work. That is a day we celebrated a huge victory, a true miracle!

With God providing the remainder of the funding we were able to complete the remodeling in six months. Key dignitaries from the city were in attendance as we held the official grand opening ceremony for the "Seed Learning Center." The vice rector of the university who originally said we would not succeed was also there!

The Seed Learning Center opened with a fully stocked library, a computer training center, and a classroom for teaching English. From the first day, hundreds came asking to be members, and the Center became a *city on a hill* whose light could not be hidden.

*Seed Learning Center Library*

Our team grew to 12 members, and we built a department around whatever skills each one brought. Out of this humble center we were able to empower local people to better themselves through books, computer training, English courses, business courses, micro credit, fruit and tomato drying projects, chicken and cow projects, and sewing courses.

The center became a place where people wanted to come and just hang out, a place where they experienced the presence of the kingdom and saw what grace actually looks like.

*Computer Lab*

We were also involved in a number of mercy projects where we helped and loved disabled orphans, provided hearing aids for the deaf, and offered pregnancy and health courses. We also ran a wrestling center for young boys from which a world champion came!

The entire center was God's idea and His doing. I look back in awe at what our team of struggling workers from around the world was able to accomplish with our love for those who have never heard the gospel.

It was such a joy to see God take our five loaves and two fish and feed the multitudes.

## POINTS TO PONDER:
- He is the God of the impossible and we need to position ourselves to see it.
- Prayer changes things.
- Jesus loves all people.
- It is truly amazing to see what He can do with a few loaves of bread and some fish.

# CHAPTER 13

# JUST AS YOU ARE

*...Everyone who calls on the name of the Lord will be saved.*

*Romans 10:13*

## September 2001

We were excited to be buying our very first house, we even had the cash in hand to pay for it—$1,500! It was hard to imagine since our car had cost double the price of the house. Where else in the world was this possible? We disregarded the old saying, "you only get what you pay for" and were only too pleased to have a place to make our own.

*Our First Home*

It was in a close-knit neighborhood and we were able to make friends with the people on our street. Odil and Nigora were wonderful neighbors and we became good friends with them. One day Nigora stopped my wife as she walked home and asked whether she fasted during the month of Ramadan. When my wife told her that we fasted and prayed many times throughout the year, not just during Ramadan, Nigora asked whether we were Christians. My wife said that we were and Nigora shared that she was a believer as well. There was an instant bond between them and they began to meet together on a regular basis to talk about issues of faith. She asked us to pray for Odil's salvation, adding that he was a great guy, but that he had some issues, alcohol being a major one.

He was a well educated man who could hold his own on any topic of conversation. We longed for him to come to faith. My parents came to visit for a week, and as always, it was a joy to take them to visit our friends. The culture has a deep respect for older people, and having my parents with us opened doors for many opportunities.

*Mom & Dad*

My father has a wonderful testimony of coming to faith, so I set up a time for us to visit with Odil. Dad agreed to tell his story while I translated. One of the main obstacles in my father's coming to faith was the idea that he was not good enough and that until he was able to change he would not be acceptable to God or ever expect to find salvation.

As my father shared the wonderful truth that you come to God as you are and that He changes you, something started to resonate in Odil's heart. He had seen an incredible change in Nigora and desperately wanted what she had found, but didn't think that he was worthy. He had been trying to change but found himself failing again and again. That night was the start of Odil's journey to seeing the Saviour who takes us as we are.

Not long after, we had the privilege of seeing him accept Jesus as his Saviour. This family became precious to us and we grieved the day we had to say goodbye.

In this part of the world people struggle through the hardships of life, but Nigora stands as a beacon of light in the darkness as she drinks from the fountain of living water that never runs dry.

## Points To Ponder:

- Jesus gave His life for sinners, not saints.
- A life surrendered to Jesus is the start of an amazing transformation.
- When a wife or husband lives out the reality of Jesus, they don't always realize the deep impact they are having on their spouse.
- There is a huge place for retired people to serve in the Muslim world.

# CHAPTER 14

# THE WEEKEND THAT CHANGED EVERYTHING

*Do not conform any longer to the pattern of this world, but be transformed by the renewing of your mind. Then you will be able to test and approve what God's will is—his good, pleasing and perfect will.*

*Romans 12:2*

## May 2003

Dilshod came to my house and asked if we could talk. He was one of the local pastors we were working with.

He was serving faithfully and sacrificially in our city but was facing a major problem. The pastors were struggling with demons that were manifesting during their meetings; he asked what they must do to get rid of them.

This was not a subject covered in our pre-field training manual and nobody on our team was experienced with it. I had some previous encounters with this back home but didn't feel confident to step into this space.

I realized that our team needed to be equipped in this area since the local leaders had nobody else to turn to. This was the beginning of an incredible journey into the area of inner healing and deliverance for me.

God brought some amazing tools our way that would ultimately revolutionize the way we would do ministry in the future. I met with other church-planting team leaders in the surrounding areas and suggested we have a weekend of training for pastors and their wives in the area of inner healing and deliverance. We invited two gifted workers in this ministry to conduct the teaching. There were about 25 that came from all across the area and we were excited as the meetings began on a Friday night.

## Chapter 14: The Weekend That Changed Everything

When preparing for a large meeting of believers in a security-sensitive place there are many more logistical issues to consider. In order to protect the believers, we agreed that none of our team members living in the city would attend.

I remember it was around midnight when the trainers arrived home, they were exhausted. They said that "it felt like the gathering of demons!" Instead of being a time of training and equipping it became a weekend of ministry into the lives of these precious leaders who, themselves, were living with deep wounds and bondage that had never been dealt with. These were key leaders serving sacrificially and leading many to Christ, yet they lived in such wounded places themselves. It was a shocking discovery that caused us to question what we were trying to accomplish.

As foreign workers, we wanted to be sure that we were properly trained for this ministry. We organized our own weekend in order to learn more and to practice with each other. We were in for a big surprise as we soon discovered all of our own wounds and unresolved issues that we had brought with us into the field.

The next few months were spent ministering to each other so that we could receive the healing we needed in order to be free to minister to the locals. We intentionally began to deal with the baggage that we had brought into our own faith, and invited Jesus to bring healing to the places where there was deep wounding and pain.

It was a new aspect in my own faith journey as I watched Jesus come in amazing ways to set the captives free to experience the freedom that He promises we can have.

With God miraculously providing the funding we were able to start a healing center in the capital city for pastors, leaders and their wives to come find a safe place for deeper ministry.

That weekend changed the way I saw and continue to do ministry regardless of the context I find myself in.

## Points To Ponder:

- At salvation the spirit is made new, but the mind is not. The renewal of your mind is a journey that must be taken to experience the fullness God promised we can have.
- If we do not deal with the baggage we bring into our faith, we will never know true freedom.
- Demons are just the fruit; we need to get to the root.
- There is no amount of wounding or baggage that Jesus cannot heal or deliver us from.

# Chapter 15

# Grace Awakening

*It is for freedom that Christ has set us free. Stand firm, then, and do not let yourselves be burdened again by a yoke of slavery.*

*Galatians 5:1*

## July 2003

I was sitting in a room with Anwar and Bahodir, two amazing local leaders who had sacrificed much for the gospel. Bahodir had strong opinions about all things which led to a number of interesting discussions when it came to matters of faith.

I was concerned with the amount of legalism that existed in the Muslim-background churches we dealt with and was trying to convince him that the church needed to focus more on grace. Grace was a term that didn't even exist in their language and a concept that was hard to grasp since they had come from a religion based completely on law.

Bahodir felt that I was being too soft on believers, making it sound as though sin was acceptable. He pointed to Anwar and said, "Look at Anwar; he has given his life for the gospel. He sets a standard for others, and his life is an example to many!" I could tell Anwar was getting uncomfortable. Bahodir was unaware that I had been meeting with Anwar for a number of weeks concerning deep issues that had led to some very unhealthy patterns in his life.

During one of our meetings Anwar had told me that while visiting with groups of believers he would experience a manifestation of demons that would attach themselves to him. When he returned home he assumed that it was part of the sacrificial ministry. We had some huge breakthroughs together and, in me, he found a safe place where he could deal with his guilt and shame, and not feel judged.

## Chapter 15: Grace Awakening

I realized that this was one of the most important gifts we were able to bring to this part of the world—a safe, non-judgmental context that enabled believers to deal with their issues. In this way, they were able to experience some of the freedom Christ says we can have. Through the grace they experienced, they were then able to become that same refuge for others. We found this to be the case even with non-believers who confided in us. Bahodir was such an influential leader, and I longed for him to experience this in his own life so that the yoke of slavery to the law could be broken.

Three years passed, and by then we were serving in a neighboring country and had little contact with him. One morning at the office I was told that there was someone wanting to see me. It was Bahodir! How he found me I'll never know! He said he was forced to leave the country and was now serving among an unreached group of illiterate gypsies in Russia. We talked at length the next day. This man of God had poured out all the guilt and shame that had built up and held him captive for so long. We sat and wept as he allowed the sweet grace of Jesus to enter in and bring deep cleansing to his heart. It was an incredible experience. The next day, he began the long journey back to serve among one of the most forgotten people on the planet… it was an emotional farewell!

## Points To Ponder:

- Grace is the breath of the kingdom of God.
- Grace sets us free from guilt and shame.
- Grace defines what Jesus did at the cross.
- A grace awakening allows us to live fully and love freely.

# Chapter 16

# Seventy Times Seven

*Jesus answered, "I tell you, not seven times, but seventy times seven."*

Matthew 18:22

## July 2004

There was a knock at our door; it was Gulia, the daughter of a local pastor. She was crying when she came in and we noticed her arms and legs were covered with cuts and her face was bruised from having been beaten. We discovered she had a problem with stealing and that this was not the first time; she had also been caught at school.

Her father decided that the only way to prevent her from stealing again was to beat her to the point that she would fear doing it again. She was a mess, and we were totally shocked. I took a picture of her and drove to her father's house to discuss it with him. I was nervous but also angry; he was a key church leader with whom we had been working.

When I showed him the photograph he was shocked that she had come to our home. I asked him if this was what the love of Jesus looked like and informed him that if he were anywhere else in the world, he would probably be in prison for this. He broke down and told me how helpless he felt and that he had tried everything, but didn't know what else to do. I told him that there was another way and asked him to promise me that he would never do it again. He and his wife agreed to let her stay with us for a week.

My wife and I prayed with her each night to try and get to the root of her problem. We discovered things that were said and done to her as a child that were driving her to this behavior. While we felt we had made progress, we did not get the breakthrough we had hoped for.

Several weeks later we went away for a few days. When we returned we found that our house had been broken into and things stolen. Our neighbors insisted that we involve the police, but as we began to put the pieces together we realized that it had to have been someone who knew us. It turned out that it was in fact Gulia.

It was easy to feel disappointment, considering all we had invested in her. Yet, when you understand the source of the behavior your ability to forgive again is much easier. Stealing was her way of easing the pain of being wounded. This was a great opportunity for us to model forgiveness to her father and mother.

We arranged for her to visit the healing center we established in the capital city. She would be ministered to by gifted women in her own language.

She returned home transformed, with a new ability to make good choices, and for that we give praise to God! She went on to marry a wonderful Christian man and is now a mother. Last I heard, they continue serve faithfully in a church located in a place that continues to be very hostile to Christians.

## Points To Ponder:

- The offender usually acts out of his or her own unresolved wounding. Knowing this makes forgiving much easier.
- Choosing to forgive brings incredible freedom to everyone involved.
- Healing is a journey that does not happen in a single night.
- Healer, Restorer, Redeemer…Jesus!

# Chapter 17

# They Walk With God

*"In the same way, let your light shine before men, that they may see your good deeds and praise your Father in heaven."*

*Matthew 5:16*

## AUGUST 2004

We had become good friends with a wonderful local family in our neighborhood and enjoyed some interesting discussions about faith. Our team was the only source of the gospel they had.

As foreigners, we knew we were being watched, so we always did our best to try and live out our faith as an example to those around us. We hoped that God would somehow use these broken vessels to reflect something of Him.

*Dignitaries from the Deaf School*

A donor had provided us with over a hundred hearing aids for the local deaf school. The mother of our neighboring family helped us make contact with the school and accompanied us the morning we went to deliver the hearing aids. There was a meal before the official

## Chapter 17: They Walk With God

presentation and we sat around a table with the head of the school and a few local dignitaries. After a few minutes the head of the school asked if we were Muslim. Silence fell, and all eyes were on us. As I tried to work out the best way to respond, the woman with us spoke up. She said, "These people walk with God. They pray to Him and live godly lives...." She went on to say things about us that we could never have said ourselves. That day she presented something of the gospel in a special way; it was a sweet moment for us.

Oftentimes I would get discouraged in our work there, wondering whether we would ever see a breakthrough for the kingdom or if we were really making a difference. That day we realized that we were living among these people as a light in the darkness, and no matter how weak we felt, we were to always make whatever effort necessary in order to be good witnesses.

God in His grace was showing Himself to these people in ways we didn't even realize. We had the opportunity to show this family the *Jesus* film, which was an experience in itself. We watched them wrestle with the truth of who Jesus really is. I wish I could say we were able to lead the entire family to salvation, but that did not happen during our time there. I trust that our witness was enough for them to find the Messiah in the days ahead, and that remains our prayer. What a delight it will be if we meet them around the throne one day.

## POINTS TO PONDER:

- A city on a hill cannot be hidden.
- Just having light is enough to make a difference to darkness.
- Our lives may be the only gospel some people ever get to see.
- When people leave my presence, does something of Jesus go with them?

# CHAPTER 18

# A REFUGEE IN TURKEY

*I can do everything through him who gives me strength.*

*Philippians 4:13*

## October 2004

I was attending a leadership conference in Turkey at the same time my visa was up for renewal for the country we were working in. The organization I worked for assured me that I would be able to renew it at the airport on my return trip. With that assurance, I left for the conference without giving it another thought.

After a great conference I went to the airport to return to my family but was informed that I would not be allowed to board the plane without a visa number. When I contacted my organization they informed me that the government had begun a plan to remove all Christian workers from the country, and that there would be no visa number... I would not be allowed to board the plane.

This was the beginning of a two-month ordeal of being stranded in Turkey without a visa. I was not allowed to return home to my family, and they were not allowed to leave the country without a valid visa.

Once again we found ourselves in new territory on this journey of faith. Day after day, week after week, we heard the same answer... no visa! Dealing with bad news on a daily basis is tough when you are told that it could be the next day, then the next. Each day it was the same story. At some point you just want to give up.

## CHAPTER 18: A REFUGEE IN TURKEY

It was difficult to wait it out, but I was now facing a bigger problem—my two-week Turkish visa was going to expire in seven days.

I spent my days in Istanbul trying to work out how to extend my visa. I hired a Turkish man to go to the international police station with me in order to obtain an extension. The place had such a bad reputation that foreigners avoided it.

I took a boat trip across the Bosphorus, a strait that forms part of the boundary between Europe and Asia, and two trams to get there, only to discover that it was closed for the day! All the effort spent hiring someone to escort me there for nothing. "God, what am I to do?"

God does have a sense of humor, though, because the only book I was able to find at the place where I was staying was *The Hiding Place* by Corrie ten Boom. It's a book about her time in Nazi prison camps. So whenever I wanted to have a pity party the book would spoil it. Corrie's sister Betsy became an example to me of how to live in the kingdom regardless of circumstances. I sensed that was what God wanted me to learn during this experience.

Time was running short so I decided to return to the police station myself the next day. I resolved that I was not going to leave until I had somehow secured an extension. When I arrived the situation was chaotic—with people from what seemed like every country frantically trying to stay in Turkey. I was handed a number and sent from one station to another, standing in many different lines. I had no idea how the system worked and struggled to find anyone who could speak English. I was clueless!

It was 4:00 p.m. and had made no progress. The police station closed at 5:00 p.m. and time was running out. I sat with my head in my hands, feeling hopeless. Suddenly I heard a voice say, "Where are you from? You look like you could use some help." I looked up to see a **young Turkish man** standing before me speaking perfect English. He was unshaven and wearing a big, dirty coat. When I explained my dilemma, he believed me and offered to help. "Follow me," he said. He then proceeded to walk straight into the main policeman's office with my passport and ask for assistance. When the policeman saw that it was a South African passport, he threw it back and told him to get out. The timing couldn't have been worse; considering that Nelson Mandela had just spoken out against the Turkish treatment of the Kurds, straining relations between the two countries. Undeterred, he walked out and told me to follow him upstairs. He walked right into the Chief Policeman's office. I could not bring myself to go in, so I waited outside the door. There was a lot of heated discussion, but five minutes later, he walked out with a signed piece of paper.

He took me to the front of the line and handed the paper to the clerk. Within five minutes I had a document stating that my extension would be ready in five days, the same day my current visa was set to expire. It was now 5:00 p.m.... closing time.

I kept wondering who this guy was. It was during Ramadan, so I traveled back with him and we broke the fast together. We spent three hours discussing faith and who God is. I discovered that he had previously lived in Austria and experienced similar difficulties with his own visa; that's why he wanted to help. He was unemployed and living in a caravan. He was a Nakshabandi, a charismatic sect of Islam birthed out of the country I was working in. We parted ways and hoped to see each other again. I went to sleep that night wondering whether it could have been an angel in disguise. Once again God showed up at five minutes to midnight in a way I could never have imagined.

## POINTS TO PONDER:

- In Philippians 4, Paul speaks of being content in every circumstance. The life of Betsy ten Boom testifies that it is possible even in the worst of circumstances.
- With God, all things are possible.
- As it was with Abraham, so it is with us: God wants us to trust Him until the stroke of midnight.
- I can do all things through Christ who gives me strength. It's about enduring through all circumstances.

# Five Minutes To Midnight

I kept wondering who this guy was. He was during Ramadan, so I traveled back with him, and we broke the fast together. We sat in their home, the name Fifi, and who died is. I discovered that he had previously lived in Austria and experienced similar difficulties with his own visa, that's why he wanted to help. He was a complete and home in a canteen. He was a Kazakhstan, charismatic sort of Islam birthed out of the country. I was wrestling on. We parted ways and hoped to see each other again. I went to sleep that night wondering what it could have been, he assumed in its grace. Once again God showed up, at five minutes to midnight in a way I could never have imagined.

## POINTS TO PONDER:

* In Philippians 4, Paul speaks of being content in every circumstance. The life of boys Ton Boom testifies that it is possible even in the worst of circumstances.

* With God, all things are possible.

* As it was with Abraham, so it is with me. God wants us to trust Him until the stroke of midnight.

* I can do all things through Christ who gives me strength. He also endures through all circumstances.

# CHAPTER 19

# THE NOVICE SMUGGLER

*God is our refuge and strength, an ever-present help in trouble.*

*Psalm 46:1*

# November 2004

My Turkish adventure had left me a little tired, plus I was recovering from a case of influenza. I missed my family and wondered when I would be able to see them again.

I was unable to return to the country my family was in, and expired visas prevented them from leaving. Rather than wait in Turkey to be reunited with them, I obtained a visa for a different Central Asian country and made plans to travel there. I was scheduled to assume a leadership role there, as well as in a large neighboring country.

I would be traveling with part of our team to visit with some of the workers there. We also decided to take some Bibles and other literature in with us. This would be my first experience in doing anything like this, and can honestly say that I was not feeling up to the task either physically or spiritually.

We filled our luggage with books and boarded the plane. There were four of us traveling together, but agreed that once we landed we would be on our own until we cleared customs. That way if anyone was caught and detained the others would not be implicated.
We landed at midnight, collected our luggage and proceeded to the customs area where our bags would be x-rayed.

I was the last of our group to be checked. Everyone else in the group made it through with no trouble. I could feel my heart

## CHAPTER 19: THE NOVICE SMUGGLER

starting to beat faster and recall praying "Okay Lord, this is where you need to make the security officials blind to the books".

As I picked up my bags to head to the exit, I felt a tap on my shoulder. It was an official motioning for me to me to open them up! I can still see the other members of my group looking nervously through a window on the outside. I remember thinking *"God, there are more books than clothes. How are you going to make them invisible?"*

I opened the bags and began to unpack the books onto the table. I put on a face of innocence—one that said, "Is there a problem here?" None of the officials could speak English, but I could tell one of them was angry. He led me into a room and made me surrender my passport.

He made a phone call and began reading from one of the Bibles to the person on the other end of the line. Clearly they were trying to determine what kind of book it was. In thinking back, even though my situation looked grim, there was a strange sense of peace that came over me. Just then a **plainclothes man** came into the room, sat with me, and smiled! He held up the books and said, "No take into our country, okay?" He handed my passport to me and said, "Go!" I thanked him and got out of there as fast as I could while the other man was still on the phone. The sense of relief was indescribable. My first thought was to wonder how many disguises these angels have. It turned out to be a very good trip, and I was glad to meet all the saints working on the frontlines.

While I was there, I received news that my family had not been able to secure visas for the country I was in. This was devastating because I was so sure we would be able to see each other when I got back.

We discovered that visas were not required for the UK, where my brother-in-law lived. So we made plans to travel there and for our flights to arrive on the same day; we would meet each other there.

I arrived in London ahead of my family and met up with my brother-in-law. Their flight was scheduled to arrive within the hour... but would they be on it? I hadn't heard whether they had made it through immigration with their expired visas on the other side.

Finally my anticipation was put to rest; the image of them coming through the doors at Heathrow airport with our two-year old daughter sitting on the luggage is forever etched in my memory.

Our two-month ordeal was finally over, and how sweet it was to be together again. I wouldn't let either of them out of my sight. I remember how my daughter sat on my lap on the way home touching my face as we got to know each other again. The feelings of joy and relief were amazing and once again our Father saw us through it all.

## Chapter 19: The Novice Smuggler

## Points to Ponder:

- Don't wait for a crisis to appreciate what you have in your family.
- Family is a treasure never to be taken for granted.
- There is a peace and confidence that God provides when you are about His business that you cannot know before you are in it.
- Some people need to get caught with Bibles; otherwise how else will the police ever hear the gospel?

# FIVE MINUTES TO MIDNIGHT

## POINTS TO PONDER:

- Don't wait for a male to appreciate who you have to your family.
- Family is a treasure never to be taken for granted.
- There is a peace and confidence that God provides when you are about His business that you cannot know before walking in it.
- Some people need to get caught with Hitler, otherwise how else will the police ever hear the proper?

# CHAPTER 20

# WAITING IS THE HARDEST PART

*Wait for the LORD; be strong and take heart and wait for the LORD.*

*Psalm 27:14*

## November 2004 - My Wife's Perspective:

Each day we were assured that Andy's visa would be granted the very next day, and each day those hopes faded away while we waited for him to return home to Central Asia.

After two long months we both agreed that I should pack up our home and try to meet each other in another country. It was distressing to our local friends, too, because they were not able to say goodbye to Andy. Many sad farewells ensued.

The local believers we had been working with so closely gathered together for a farewell party, where they videotaped their messages to him.

With a downcast heart and our two year old in tow, I made my way to the capital city to depart. We passed through numerous military checkpoints along the way, one of which proved particularly difficult to negotiate without a current visa.

Explaining our situation was fruitless, and nothing I said would convince them to allow us to go on. We were told repeatedly to turn around and go home.

## Chapter 20: Waiting Is The Hardest Part

I was desperate; having been forcibly separated from my husband for such a long period and now being told I couldn't leave the country to be with him. I broke down and sobbed in the taxi.

*Stephanie Wiping Mommy's Tears*

As my daughter gently wiped the tears from my cheeks, the taxi driver said that he would go speak to the police for me. It seemed like hours before he came back to the car and said we were clear to go through. I was filled with joy and grateful to him for whatever he did or said to help us.

We inched our way closer to the capital city, hopeful that we would soon be reunited with Andy. But that was short-lived.

I was pulled aside while checking through at the airport and told that I would not be able to leave because of my expired visa. I felt trapped, but looking at my daughter's calm and trusting face I knew that I had to trust in my Father with this situation too!

My brother-in-law was with me and saw the desperation in my eyes. He said to wait while he spoke with the officials. Again the waiting seemed like hours and I could feel the hope of seeing my husband slipping away.

My brother-in-law was able to persuade the official and I finally received word that I could check through to the plane. Walking through the airport gates felt like leaving prison, but I was not going to get my hopes up this time until the plane actually took off with us on board!

Waiting is a difficult test of our faith. While I waited, I tried to cast my anxiety on God and trust Him with our circumstance.

Chapter 20: Waiting Is The Hardest Part

Eventually we boarded the plane and took off. My anxiety now turned to anticipation as my daughter and I talked about seeing her daddy again.

*A Happy Reunion*

What a joy to be greeted by Andy at the airport on the other side and to know that we would be able to travel to our home country together!

## POINTS TO PONDER:

- God's timing is always right and usually different from ours.
- He is the author of true ministry and decides when our part in it is over.
- God uses children to teach us about Himself.
- Waiting on Him when there is nothing else you can do is one of the hardest acts of faith.

# CHAPTER 21

# GETTING TO THE OTHER SIDE

*I will lie down and sleep in peace, for you alone, O LORD, make me dwell in safety.*

Psalm 4:8

## April 2005

I woke up early in the morning knowing it was going to be a day we would not forget! We were moving to a neighboring country where I was to begin a regional leadership role in our organization. All of our belongings were stowed in 25 bags and thus began the arduous attempt of crossing from one Central Asian country into another.

Our first child was two years old, and my wife was seven months pregnant. We loaded our luggage into an old Russian truck and headed for the border at the mercy of an unknown driver. The thought of what lay ahead had me on my knees begging God to go before us.

Each bag was labeled with its contents in hopes of satisfying the border officials so they wouldn't want to go through and inspect each bag. In this part of the world it's not uncommon for police and corruption to go hand in hand, and you can pretty much count on them coming up with a reason to extort money from you. Foreigners are always treated with suspicion and I knew there would be no way for us to simply cross the border under the radar.

Our driver sensed our anxiety and said he knew of another border crossing that he thought would be less problematic in getting us across. So off we went, all squashed into the front seat of this old truck. We couldn't wait for the end of the day when we hoped to get a good nights rest on the other side of the border. We arrived at the small border post almost two hours later. The driver went to

## Chapter 21: Getting To The Other Side

speak with the officials, when they learned we were foreigners they refused us entry and told us to go back to the main border crossing. This little excursion had added more than three hours to our journey.

We arrived at the border as thousands of people were coming and going by foot, car, bus, and bicycle. We were stopped and the officials began looking through our bags. They called me into the office and asked for a document that declared the amount of money I had brought into the country the last time I flew in. This procedure had been curtailed at the airports months earlier, so I had nothing to show them. I tried explaining the situation to them but they would not listen. They said that unless I could produce the paperwork they would not let us through. I knew they were after a bribe, but not sure how much.

I went over to my wife and explained the situation; together we concocted a *Hollywood performance* plan and hoped for the best. She got out of the car and I proceeded to explain what we would have to do. We spoke in the local language. I told her that it would be necessary for me to leave her and our daughter alone there while I returned to try and locate a document that I knew didn't exist. My wife began crying and asked in a louder than usual voice; "How can you leave us? Where will we go? What if something happens to us?" I pointed toward the border officials and said, "If anything happens to you then these people will have to answer for that!" That exchange, together with a hot, exhausted and sobbing wife and young child seemed to have an effect on them. They took pity on us and said "okay, okay, just get in the truck and go!" So that's exactly what we did.

Four hours later we arrived in a city on the other side, where some fellow workers took us in for the night. We went to bed exhausted, but rejoicing knowing that we were safe and that we had not lost a single bag. Once again our Father had seen us through a tough day, and a new chapter in our journey was set to begin.

## POINTS TO PONDER:

- His faithfulness is not always wrapped up in bows, but He IS faithful!
- There is a place in the kingdom for playacting.
- The mountain always looks intimidating before you cross, but once you are on the other side you can look back in amazement at how He got you there.
- The safest place to be is in the hands of the Father.

# CHAPTER 22

# OUR CENTRAL ASIAN CHILD

*the LORD was with him; he showed him kindness and granted him favor in the eyes of the prison warden.*

*Genesis 39:21*

## August 2005

The time had arrived for our second child to make her entry into the world. In Central Asia we were aware of only one medical clinic with a maternity unit run by an American doctor. It was located in the country we had just left a few months earlier which meant we would have to travel back for the birth. We had confidence in the doctor and trusted the delivery would be a safe one.

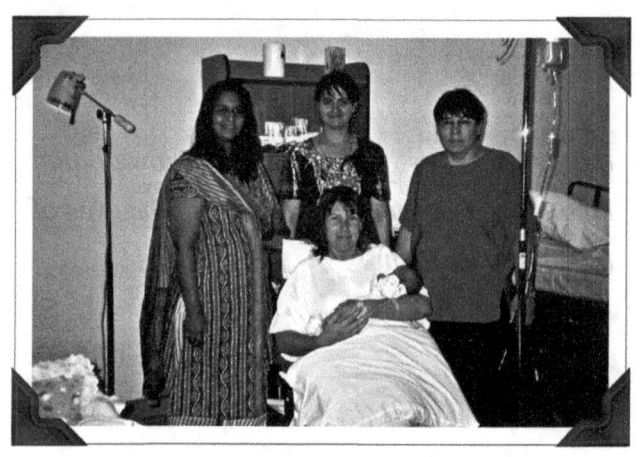

*A Safe Delivery*

A friend from our home country was prepared to help; she was a very experienced midwife. We were grateful for her offer and gladly accepted. We knew ahead of time that the birth would be by C-section and arranged for an Indian surgeon to operate. Everything went smoothly—just as was planned—and on that day, around 10:00 a.m., Rebecca Grace entered the world in the presence of an

## CHAPTER 22: OUR CENTRAL ASIAN CHILD

American Mormon doctor, an Indian Hindu surgeon, a South African Christian midwife, a Russian Orthodox nurse, a Central Asian Muslim assistant, and a bewildered father! It was an amazing day!

My wife had labored through her hard work; now mine was about to begin. Rebecca was registered as being born in this Central Asian country, but we needed to have her registered as a citizen of our home country and obtain a passport for her. There was no embassy nearby; the closest one was in Turkey, quite a long way away. We needed pictures for her passport, so with Rebecca only three hours old, we held her up and asked her to smile for the camera. Needless to say, a number of photos were taken during that photo shoot!

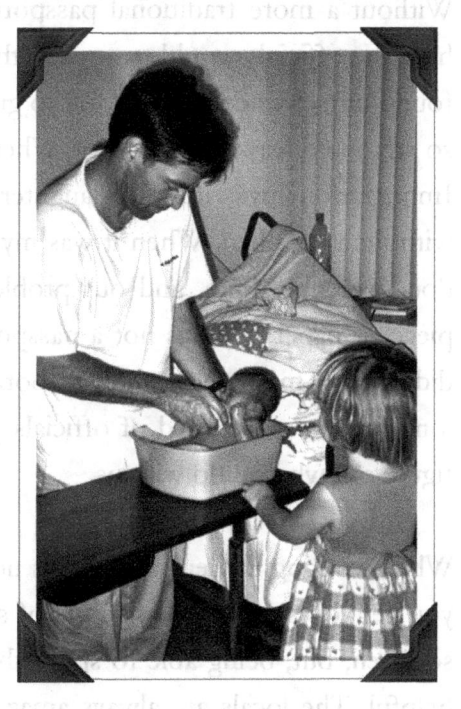

*Dad & Stef Meeting Becky*

Our travel visas were good for one month so time was an issue. We gathered Rebecca's photos and other necessary documentation and faxed them to the embassy in Turkey for processing. They happily issued her an identity number and temporary passport; it was a simple piece of paper with her photograph and an official stamp on it.

Without a more traditional passport we were nervous about how the officials would treat us at the airport and, once again, found ourselves calling on God to grant us favor at the airport so we could leave the country. When we got to Customs and Immigration my wife and daughter Stephanie went through without a problem. When it was my turn, I handed Rebecca's documents to them, and our problems began. "What is this piece of paper? This is not a passport! Where is her visa?" It didn't even matter that she was born in their country! Before long there was a crowd of officials gathered around trying to figure out what to do with us.

While working in Central Asia it's not uncommon to ask how you get yourself into these sorts of situations since it happens so often, but, being able to speak the local language is always helpful. The locals are always amazed that a foreigner would take the time to learn their language.

## Chapter 22: Our Central Asian Child

With my wife and Stephanie standing on one side of immigration, their passports already exit stamped, and me standing on the other side with Rebecca, I began to explain. It seemed like an eternity, but I was finally able to persuade them that the documents were, in fact, valid. After hearing the sweet sound of the exit stamp we were on our way—to the plane, that is! We were not out of the woods yet; we still needed to re-enter our country of residence with these same documents.

I'm not sure what to write on a visa application form for an infant when it asks to state "purpose of visit," but our three-week-old baby needed to have one in order to get into the country. When we landed we were fortunate to have a very good agent who was able to speak with the immigration people by telephone. They immediately issued Rebecca a visa number. With an embassy located in this country we were able to follow up and get a proper ID book and passport for her.

So we survived the birth of our Central Asian child... but just barely!

## Points To Ponder:
- God can persuade people in power to show favor to His own.
- Learning the local language always pays off.
- When things are out of our control, He is faithful and in control!
- Children are a gift from God.

# Chapter 23

# Up In Smoke

*But store up for yourselves treasures in heaven, where moth and rust do not destroy, and where thieves do not break in and steal.*

*Matthew 6:20*

## January 2006

January 6, 2006, 10:00 o'clock in the morning and -25 degrees Celsius—a date, time and temperature I will never forget.

We were running a pretty big operation out of our offices, managing two non-government organizations (NGO) and a recording studio. We performed Bible translation work there and also ran a literature distribution center; all while serving 70 workers in four countries

On that day our office manager ran in white-faced shouting that there was a fire! When I looked through to the stairwell I could see that the flames were already three meters high. There had been an electrical fault, and the accommodation area, made entirely of wood, was now ablaze.

Our top priority and biggest challenge was to get everyone safely out of the building, which was three stories tall. We ran through the building shouting for everyone to get out. Thankfully everyone escaped to safety.

We stood helpless and watched as the fire engulfed one whole section. We waited for what seemed like an eternity before the fire department arrived, only to watch in disbelief as they tried using a hose with little to no water pressure.

## Chapter 23: Up In Smoke

Eventually a larger vehicle arrived and the brave fire fighters began the battle of getting the fire under control and extinguished. They were especially brave since their uniforms were not exactly state of the art.

One image I still have in my mind is of one of the fire fighters taking a smoke break on the roof while the fire raged behind him. It was surreal. The water flowing from the roof was actually freezing before it even reached the ground. I was in shock and disbelief, hoping that we might wake up from this nightmare.

Suddenly my adrenalin level dropped and realized that I was shivering. I was wearing only a shirt and the temperature was -25 degrees Celsius. We decided to take turns sitting in a running car to try and stay warm.

Our hearts sank as we watched the fire move to the office area where we stored critical files and information, computers and $50,000 in the safe. The saddest thought, however, was of the years of Bible translation work that sat on one of the laptop computers. "Please help us, Lord" was all we could pray.

The fire was finally put out around 4:00 p.m., which gave us about an hour to rummage through what was left to try and salvage what we could. Whatever was left would be at risk of being stolen or frozen overnight.

*Fire Damage*

So began the miracles! We removed the safe and took it to one of the worker's homes. When we opened it we found $50,000 floating in water. As we laid hundred-dollar bills out to dry on the apartment floor, I remember thinking that now I can say that I have been involved in a money laundering operation.

The laptops were singed and blackened, but somehow the hard drives were in complete working condition with all the translation work saved. In fact all of the important files were recovered without losing a single official document. The workers from the recording studio had left an envelope containing thousands of dollars next to their bed. When they cleared away the ashes, the envelope was still there with no damage to the funds. The building had been destroyed with nothing much left, and yet God had protected the things most important to us, especially those items that money could never replace.

We put together a recovery team and started a restoration fund. I was not a fundraiser and had no idea how to even begin raising the $150,000 needed to rebuild, but God did.

*New Office Building*

A fellow worker was able to provide temporary office space for us, and volunteers from Scotland arrived to help us rebuild. They laid new foundations and installed new electrical wiring while my wife drew up plans for a new accommodation block. We redesigned the office area and waited on the Lord.

One year and $150,000 later we moved into the new and improved building, and as I write today, it continues to be a launching pad for ministry all over Central Asia.

## POINTS TO PONDER:

- None of us know what each day will bring.
- Only place true value in what is irreplaceable.
- He really does own the cattle on a thousand hills.
- Out of the ashes, beauty will rise. He can turn a tragedy into a triumph.

# CHAPTER 24

# A HEALING PLANNED 100 YEARS AGO

*"Indeed, the very hairs of your head are all numbered. Don't be afraid; you are worth more than many sparrows."*

*Luke 12:7*

## April 2006

Back in 2004 we had been working with a school for the deaf and invited a **woman to help with testing** and to provide hearing aids to the children. It was a privilege to have her visit the school since she specialized in people with hearing difficulties.

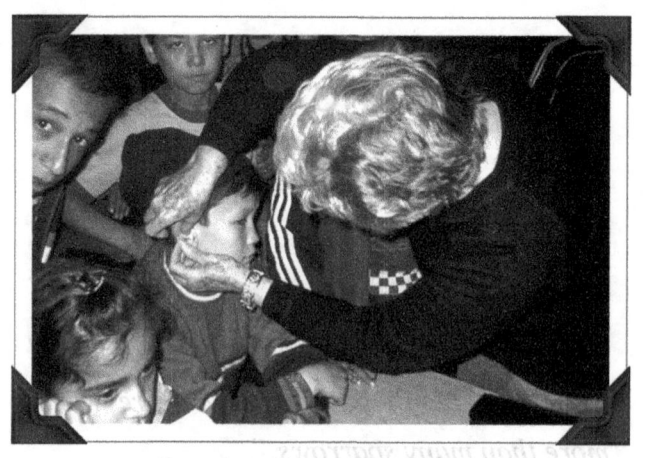

*Our Angel at the Deaf School*

She made a big difference in many of the kids' lives and, without us even realizing it, to my wife as well. While she was staying with us she tested my wife's ears and discovered that she had severe hearing loss in one of her ears. She fitted her with a hearing aid that made a difference, although it was uncomfortable.

Then in 2005 we flew home. My father-in-law set up an appointment for my wife to visit his ENT specialist to see whether more could be done to improve her hearing with a better hearing aid. When the specialist examined her he discovered that much of her inner ear had been damaged by an aggressive growth. He operated to remove the growth and then attempted to rebuild the inner ear. All seemed to go well, we were thankful and returned to the country we were serving in.

In 2007 we were invited to return home to participate in our church's centenary celebrations. We notified the specialist that we were coming, and he suggested that she have a check up as soon as we got off the plane. Any trip home was tough, usually involving 30 hours of flying and waiting at airports, plus a five-hour time change.

We landed, exhausted from traveling, with two small kids, and headed straight for the hospital. Our youngest daughter was eight months old and still breastfeeding. Following a quick feed, I left my wife at the hospital for what we expected to be a simple checkup.

We planned to stay with my wife's aunt, so I headed over to their home with the kids and crashed, expecting a wake-up call from the hospital at any moment to come pick her up. After four hours I was concerned, so I contacted the hospital. They informed me that she was still in the operating room! Eight hours later I received word that I could finally visit her.

When I saw her, there were bandages covering her entire head. I was shocked. In the process of checking her ear the doctor discovered that the growth had returned and become aggressive. It was dangerously close to affecting her brain.

My wife spent the night in the hospital and was not able to feed Rebecca due to the anesthetic and medication in her system. I was facing the daunting task of watching over our little one, who, until now, had never spent a night without mom. I could not imagine how we were going to get through the night. Exhausted from traveling plus the stress of the day's activities, I was hoping we could just collapse into our beds and sleep.

My wife's aunt was an angel and a great help; she prepared a bottle of formula and we made it through the night. It wasn't the best night, but we survived.

My wife recovered from the surgery and we were able to return to the field a week later, though she required three follow-up checks to make sure the growth did not return. It has been almost six years since then with no sign of the growth, Jesus be praised!

Looking back we can once again see how miraculously God orchestrated a number of events that enabled my wife to continue serving Him so faithfully. A hearing aid specialist happens to test her ear; a church brings us home for a 100-year celebration; then an emergency surgery that prevents her brain from being damaged. So much to be thankful for!

## Points To Ponder:

- In the kingdom of God there is no such thing as coincidence.
- The miracle touch of God can occur at any time during the healing process.
- He knows each hair on our head.
- Mother's milk is living proof of a Creator!

## CHAPTER 25

## A DREAM COME TRUE

*"But you will receive power when the Holy Spirit comes on you; and you will be my witnesses in Jerusalem, and in all Judea and Samaria, and to the ends of the earth."*

*Acts 1:8*

## December 2006

In a joint effort with another family, we reached out to an unreached minority people group in the city we were in. They had many barriers and misconceptions about the gospel and we found them quite resistant to the message.

We felt God leading us to try something new, so we made plans for a group of Muslim-background believers we knew from the neighboring country to visit for a week to do ministry in the area. Six of them came to visit. This was the beginning of one of the most exciting ministry experiences of my life.

When it was time for them to leave, there were some new believers and a number of contacts for us to follow up with. While they were with us we were able to minister into their lives as well in order to strengthen and build up their faith. They were able to return to their country with a renewed passion after seeing how God had used them.

We saw how amazingly effective the locals were at evangelism and made plans for it to be an annual summer event. We brought them together for a few days of training and then sent them out in teams for two weeks. In the second year of this program thirty believers from all over Central Asia were recruited and sent out in five teams.

During their debriefings we heard of many Muslims being led to Christ, literature being distributed in bazaars, and *Jesus* films

## Chapter 25: A Dream Come True

distributed by the hundreds—things a foreigner could never get away with.

By the third year we had gathered 70 believers from six different cultures. Fifteen teams were sent to five different countries, reaching out to places that were completely untouched by the gospel.

Training was a very special time. Some of the workers had never seen or been with so many believers at one time, and they were greatly encouraged.

Putting teams together in the span of two days was a bit of a challenge—considering their different backgrounds, screening processes, the logistical nightmares of sending teams across borders, and arranging accommodations in illegal settings. If we had stopped to think about everything that could have gone wrong we might have gone insane. It all added up to blissful chaos and required faith to move mountains. In the midst of our poor planning God chose to bless us and our efforts; every team reported amazing results.

As I write this book the program is entering its sixth year with 25 teams sent out during the last year. Over 100 Muslims came to Christ and almost 1,000 heard the gospel message for the first time. Precious literature has been placed into the hands of thousands so that they can read the Word of God for the first time in their own language. It was also the first year in which follow-up teams were sent back to return to those places where there had been fruit in order to establish house churches. We have even begun to see some of those who came to Christ from the first outreach now going out as missionaries visiting the unreached in other countries.

This was something I had dreamed of but never imagined would become a reality. How wonderful it is to see a heart for missions being part of the DNA of the early church that is still being birthed in Central Asia.

## POINTS TO PONDER:
- Reaching all peoples with the gospel is HIS mission and He is doing it.
- "Expect great things from God, attempt great things for God" ~ William Carey
- His Body is united through missions, and He gets the glory.
- Missions is a mandate for every church, no matter how young or how large.

# CHAPTER 26

# LOVE IS A VERB

*Do nothing out of selfish ambition or vain conceit, but in humility consider others better than yourselves. Each of you should look not only to your own interests, but also to the interests of others.*

*Philippians 2:3-4*

## December 2007

Over the years my wife had been discipling three local women. They were reading through *The Purpose Driven Life* by Rick Warren together and came across the chapter on love. While discussing what love in action really looks like, they were interrupted by a loud banging on the door. A young mother whom my wife knew came running into our courtyard carrying her infant son. She hurriedly handed her baby over to my wife briefly explaining that she urgently needed to go see someone. She asked whether my wife could please look after her baby until she got back. Without waiting for a reply she ran off with no estimate of when she would return leaving my wife quite dazed.

The women continued the lesson on love with my wife now cradling an infant in her arms. They were discussing what it meant to lay down your life for another when the baby began to wriggle and cry. The lesson was cut short and the other women left.

My wife thought that the time spent together had been unfruitful and considered it a waste of time. Soon the time came for us to move to a neighboring country and we lost contact with many of the locals we had grown to know and love. One day we received news that Jamila, one of the three ladies, was working in a huge outdoor bazaar in the city we were living in. After some effort we found where she was staying and went to see how she was doing. It was a cold night and we trudged through dark and muddy alleys carrying our two little kids, wondering if we would ever find her.

## Chapter 26: Love Is A Verb

After almost an hour we located where she was staying and entered a 5 x 3 foot room with only a mattress on the floor. There was a place to make tea, but there was no heat. She was sitting on the mattress when we walked in. It was difficult seeing her like this.

Her eyes lit up when she saw us and we had a sweet reunion. She had come to work in this country in an attempt to earn money to feed her family back home. In the midst of all of this hardship she had a joy in her eyes that defied explanation; it was the presence of God with her there.

As we sat and reminisced about the past, she reminded my wife of the studies they did together, especially the incident with the infant. The idea of someone accepting the care of a baby like my wife did was something totally foreign in the local culture. Normally the mother would have been given a harsh scolding. For Jamila, the fact that my wife had *laid down her plans* for the day was one of the greatest lessons in love she had learned.

At the time we left that country, Jamila was one of the key leaders in the work there. When we found her we were concerned because, instead of serving the new church in her own country, she was in another country striving to keep her family alive

We felt she had a calling and anointing on her life for ministry. We worked with our team to create a support budget for her and, with great joy, commissioned her back so she could continue her church-planting efforts among her own people.

We got to see her every year after that when she brought others to participate in our summer outreaches and when hosting teams came to her city.

## Points To Ponder:
- God uses everything, even that which we would consider a "waste of time."
- Daily life is the canvas for discipleship.
- How you react to a disruption in your daily plans speaks truth.
- He watches over those who are His.

# CHAPTER 27

# WHO ARE YOU?

*He rescued me from my powerful enemy,*
*from my foes, who were too strong for me.*
*They confronted me in the day of my disaster,*
*but the LORD was my support.*

*Psalm 18:17-18*

## July 2008

I crossed over the border to visit some of our workers in another country in Central Asia. I was asked to take two boxes of literature, written in the local language, back to my country for distribution. The books were legal in the country I was visiting and knew that the border guards rarely checked all the cars coming through, so I agreed.

In order to get a taxi, you need to visit a reserved area where drivers hold up signs with the names of cities that they are driving to. Once you negotiate a seat and the car is full, you are on your way. I decided not to let the driver know about the books, thinking it would just complicate matters; plus I wasn't sure anyone would want to take me if they knew.

It was an hour drive from the capital to the border, then another four hours to my home city. At the border, passengers exit to walk through customs while the taxis go another way.

Once through customs I was not able locate my taxi with my computer still in it. I wondered whether my driver might have taken off with it. My heart stopped when I finally saw it. The driver was still at the border crossing; an official was looking through the trunk. I thought *Oh Lord, please, not again!*

Twenty minutes later he came driving through fuming! He asked who I was and accused me of being a Muslim fundamentalist! (That

## CHAPTER 27: WHO ARE YOU?

is the last thing I thought I would ever be accused of.) He asked me what the books were but nothing I said would satisfy him. He had paid a rather large bribe to the official and said I would have to pay him twice the amount. So began one of the longest four hours of my life.

As we drove to the city he and the others in the car began to taunt me. After two hours he pulled the car over to a deserted area and stopped the car. He made a phone call and a few minutes later two other cars pulled up. The men got out and began going through the trunk and yelling about the books. I tried explaining that they were books that would help you in your walk with God.

One driver demanded $1,000 and said they were going to hand me over to the authorities if I didn't pay.

I decided to speak only in English so that they would not be able to communicate with me. I was very nervous. I was in a situation where these men could do whatever they wanted to me and nobody would know.

**One of the men looking at the books** suddenly spoke up and said, "Look, there is nothing wrong with these titles. They look like good books. Let him go!" It seemed to work, and miraculously we were back on the road. In my heart I was thanking God for this man.

I had arranged to be dropped off close to my home, but as we got closer the driver said he was going to drop me off at the taxi rank instead—the place from which all taxis depart and arrive. I explained to him how I had been in his country for a number of years, doing what I could to help his people, and then told him about things I struggled with.

I said, "As a Muslim you tell me you are a man of your word, yet I have found so many, like you, who say one thing and then do another. You are really just out to cheat and deceive. Is this what you want me to think of Muslims? I am a guest in your country, and you have treated me like dirt all the way here. You never even looked at the books to see that they are actually a blessing for your people!"

When we arrived at the drop-off point he got my luggage and books from the trunk. I paid him and started to walk away when he said, "Wait! Do not leave until you have forgiven me." I told him I forgave him; we hugged and parted in peace.

When I got home I collapsed into a chair, thankful to my Father for getting me through it all!

## Points To Ponder:

- Take time to pray for the many saints who transport Bibles and other literature to those desperate for it. They are placed in dangerous situations almost daily.
- In a crisis, God always seems to put someone in the crowd who is His representative. Look for that person and be at peace.
- There is a time to speak and a time to be silent.
- He gives you the words to speak when something needs to be said.

## FIVE MINUTES TO MIDNIGHT

## CHAPTER 28

# THE MACEDONIAN CALL

*During the night Paul had a vision of a man of Macedonia standing and begging him, "Come over to Macedonia and help us."*

Acts 16:9

## July 2008

As a foreigner it was difficult to travel to the country south of where we lived, especially if you were visiting on a short-term mission trip. Everyone would know about it as soon as you entered a village.

The people were desperate for the gospel, so I contacted a friend doing translation work there and asked if he could arrange a ministry for some Muslim-background believers. We wanted them to visit some villages that had never had a witness before.

With plans in place I called Mustafa and Farghod, two amazing brothers faithfully serving in their own culture and bold in their witness. I asked whether they were up for a two-week evangelism trip down south.

A few weeks later they traveled to the main city by taxi where my friend met them. When they arrived they were provided with some local clothing and then oriented to the local lifestyle. They were also given two backpacks full of literature and a phone to use in case of emergency. A taxi driver would be taking them to three different villages where foreigners had never set foot. They would blend in well there and be able to communicate effectively in their own language. They spent two weeks there.

During that time they were able to share the love of Jesus with these people who never even knew that He existed.

## Chapter 28: The Macedonian Call

Before their visit they were under the impression that their own living conditions were quite poor. However when they arrived in these villages, to them, it felt as though they were visiting a people who had been completely forgotten. It was utter poverty— illiterate people lived in clay shelters with no running water. It was a life changing experience for both of them.

At our debriefing I listened as Mustafa and Farghod tried to work through the details of how they and their own churches could make a difference for these people. Between their two congregations there were about 40 believers, all of whom were poor.

I was moved to tears as I considered the resources that the western Church has and yet unwilling to reach these forgotten people.

Mustafa then reached into his pocket and pulled out 200 passport photos that the village leaders had given them as they were leaving. As he spread them out on our kitchen table, he said that the leaders there had begged them to show the pictures to the foreigners back home in hopes that they might take pity on them.

We label these people the most resistant to the gospel message and yet, that night, I looked at the images of 200 faces desperately calling; "Will you come and rescue us?"

## Points to Ponder:

- In the Muslim world, the harvests are ripe, but workers are few.
- "We talk of the Second Coming; half the world has never heard of the first." ~ Oswald J. Smith
- God has some awesome leaders in Central Asia.
- Will you come and rescue us?

# CHAPTER 29

# WAITING ALL THIS TIME

> *"And afterward, I will pour out my Spirit on all people. Your sons and daughters will prophesy, your old men will dream dreams, your young men will see visions."*
>
> *Joel 2:28*

## July 2009

One of the joys of having indigenous believers go on mission trips is that they are able to go places that are normally restricted to foreigners.

We were involved with sending a small team of believers across the border back into their home country, where most of the inhabitants were untouched by the gospel.

Upon arrival they were given a brief orientation by our contacts in the main city along with lots of literature and train tickets.

After a long train ride they arrived in a city that was closed to foreigners and checked into a cheap hotel directly across the road from a multistory police facility.

After a day of praying through the city the workers began visiting homes. They were welcomed into the first home; the people were amazed that they had come such a long way to see them. The believers helped with the preparation of food and by the end of the day, the entire family had heard the good news! The gospel was presented to them for the first time from the mouths of their own people, and salvation came to that household that day!

The team then met up with some young people in a park who invited them into their home. Some amazing discussions about faith took place and they were able to leave behind printed copies of the gospels. As they were leaving the father of the house came out shouting and telling them to stop. The team wasn't sure what to do. The father asked where the books had come from, and that, years earlier he had a dream that someone would bring these books. He said that he had been waiting for them. Then he asked for more copies!

The team was shocked and amazed! They gave him additional copies of the gospels, then he left thankful and rejoicing. They returned with some amazing stories that were reminiscent of the book of Acts.

With a new desire to see the kingdom of God established in these places, a number of those team members hoped to return long term. It was exciting to see genuine partnerships forming between local and foreign workers, and it was just the beginning of more effective and strategic mission work to come.

## POINTS TO PONDER:

- Foreign and local missionaries working together are a powerful combination. Both are needed for the work to continue.
- God goes before us to prepare people for the gospel.
- God is raising up a whole new workforce to prepare for the harvest.

# CHAPTER 30

# ANGELS UNAWARE

*For he will command his angels concerning you to guard you in all your ways.*

Psalm 91:11

## October 2010

After leaving the mission field I signed up for a training seminar in counseling at a seminary not too far from home. During registration I was given a blanket; I couldn't help but wonder how we were going to make use of it.

During one of the evening sessions, we were asked to cover ourselves with the blanket and invite Jesus to meet us there in that place. I gave it a try and found my mind wandering off to all the difficult places and struggles I had faced during the ten years we had served in Central Asia. I found myself asking God where He had been during all those times when things didn't go well.

I was being taken on a journey, re-visiting the memories of all the places I had visited before. But this time was different. This time a particular person was being highlighted in each story I recalled. Every time an incident came to mind I felt God give me a gentle reminder. "Remember the plainclothes man with the smile when you were caught smuggling Bibles? I put him there" and "Remember the lady your mom met the night before you were going to go home because of your wife's illness? I put her there." Then there was the woman at the deaf school; God said, "I sent her as well."

## Chapter 30: Angels Unaware

God took me to each place and showed me the person He put there to get me through each situation. I don't know what angels look like or what form they take or whether people even know that God is using them to watch over His people. I only know that His eyes are always on us, and He gives His angels charge over us. I believe it, and it gives me confidence for the days ahead when my family and I will face situations where there seems to be no way out.

The time under the blanket was a healing time for me. That's when I decided to be more intentional, and began writing these stories down as a living witness of the faithfulness of our God to an ordinary family whom He loves very much.

As you have journeyed with me through these stories, you may have noticed certain people who appeared in bold type. God showed me that these were the very people whom He had placed there for us. I trust that as you look back through your own memories, you too will be able to see and testify to the presence of God in the midst of your greatest trials, because He promised that He would never leave us or forsake us.